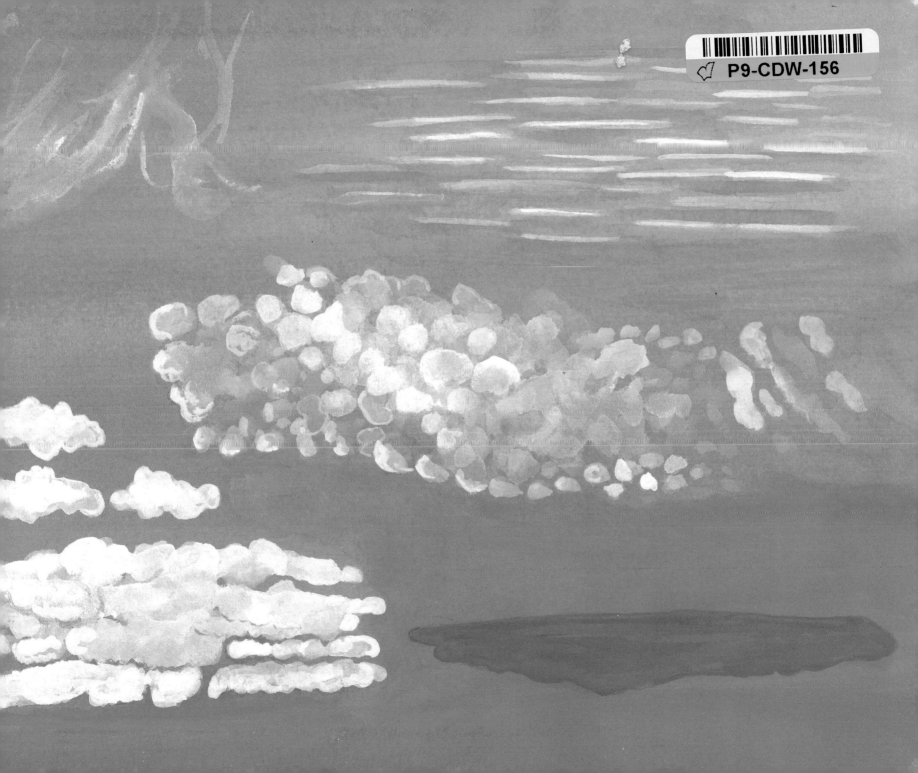

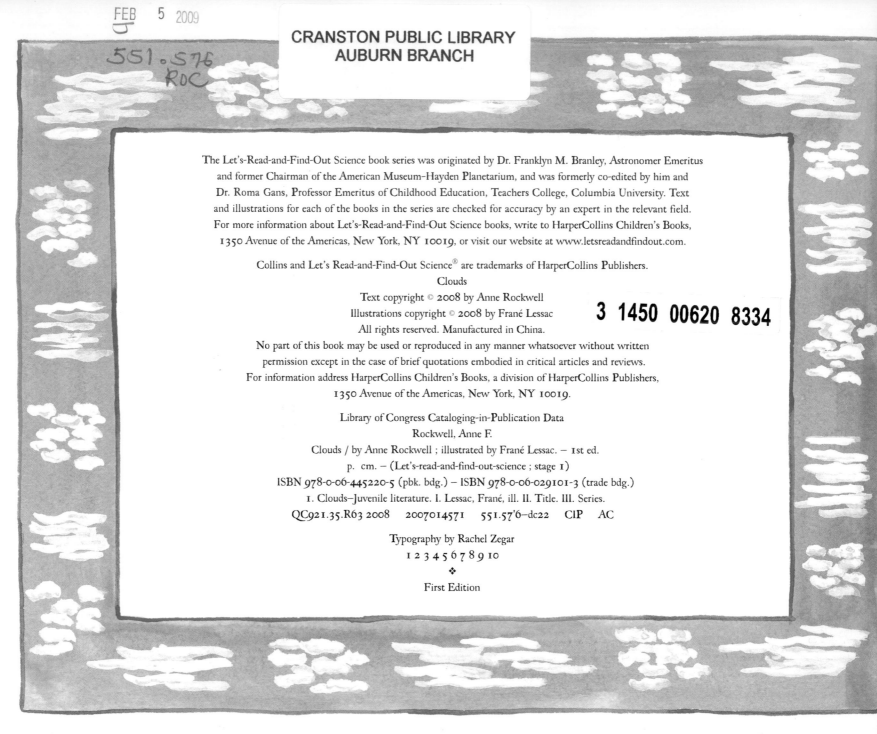

The Let's-Read-and-Find-Out Science book series was originated by Dr. Franklyn M. Branley, Astronomer Emeritus
and former Chairman of the American Museum–Hayden Planetarium, and was formerly co-edited by him and
Dr. Roma Gans, Professor Emeritus of Childhood Education, Teachers College, Columbia University. Text
and illustrations for each of the books in the series are checked for accuracy by an expert in the relevant field.
For more information about Let's-Read-and-Find-Out Science books, write to HarperCollins Children's Books,
1350 Avenue of the Americas, New York, NY 10019, or visit our website at www.letsreadandfindout.com.

Collins and Let's Read-and-Find-Out Science® are trademarks of HarperCollins Publishers.

Clouds
Text copyright © 2008 by Anne Rockwell
Illustrations copyright © 2008 by Frané Lessac
All rights reserved. Manufactured in China.
No part of this book may be used or reproduced in any manner whatsoever without written
permission except in the case of brief quotations embodied in critical articles and reviews.
For information address HarperCollins Children's Books, a division of HarperCollins Publishers,
1350 Avenue of the Americas, New York, NY 10019.

Library of Congress Cataloging-in-Publication Data
Rockwell, Anne F.
Clouds / by Anne Rockwell ; illustrated by Frané Lessac. — 1st ed.
p. cm. – (Let's-read-and-find-out-science ; stage 1)
ISBN 978-0-06-445220-5 (pbk. bdg.) – ISBN 978-0-06-029101-3 (trade bdg.)
1. Clouds–Juvenile literature. I. Lessac, Frané, ill. II. Title. III. Series.
QC921.35.R63 2008   2007014571   551.57'6–dc22   CIP   AC

Typography by Rachel Zegar
1 2 3 4 5 6 7 8 9 10
❖
First Edition

LET'S-READ-AND-FIND-OUT SCIENCE®

STAGE 1

Clouds

by Anne Rockwell

illustrated by Frané Lessac

Collins
An Imprint of HarperCollins Publishers

Look up at the sky. Do you see white or gray shapes moving across it? Those are clouds.

Most clouds are too far away to feel. You can only look at them.

But there's one kind of cloud you can feel standing on the ground. That is fog. It's the lowest kind of cloud.

You can learn a lot from looking at clouds. The shape of clouds and whether they are dark or bright can tell you how high they are and what kind of weather they will bring.

All clouds are made of water and particles of dust
too small to see.

The highest clouds are six to nine kilometers up in the sky. That is three to four miles high. It's so cold up there that all the water in those clouds freezes and becomes tiny crystals of ice.

There are three kinds of clouds high up in the atmosphere: cirrus clouds, cirrostratus clouds, and cirrocumulus clouds.

The beginning of a cloud's name tells how high up it is. The next part tells what shape it is.

Cirrostratus

Cirrus

Cirrocumulus

Cumulonimbus

Altostratus

Altocumulus

Cumulus

Stratocumulus

Nimbostratus

Stratus

Cirrus clouds are hardly there. They look like wispy white feathers trailing across blue sky. They mean sunny weather with no rain. They are far apart and let the sun shine on the earth.

Cirrostratus clouds can cover the whole sky. They tell us that it may rain or snow in twelve to twenty-four hours. "Stratus" means clouds that are flat and spread out like a blanket.

Small, puffy white clouds scattered across the entire sky are cirrocumulus clouds. "Cumulus" means that a cloud is rounded instead of flat. Cirrocumulus clouds can mean it's going to get colder.

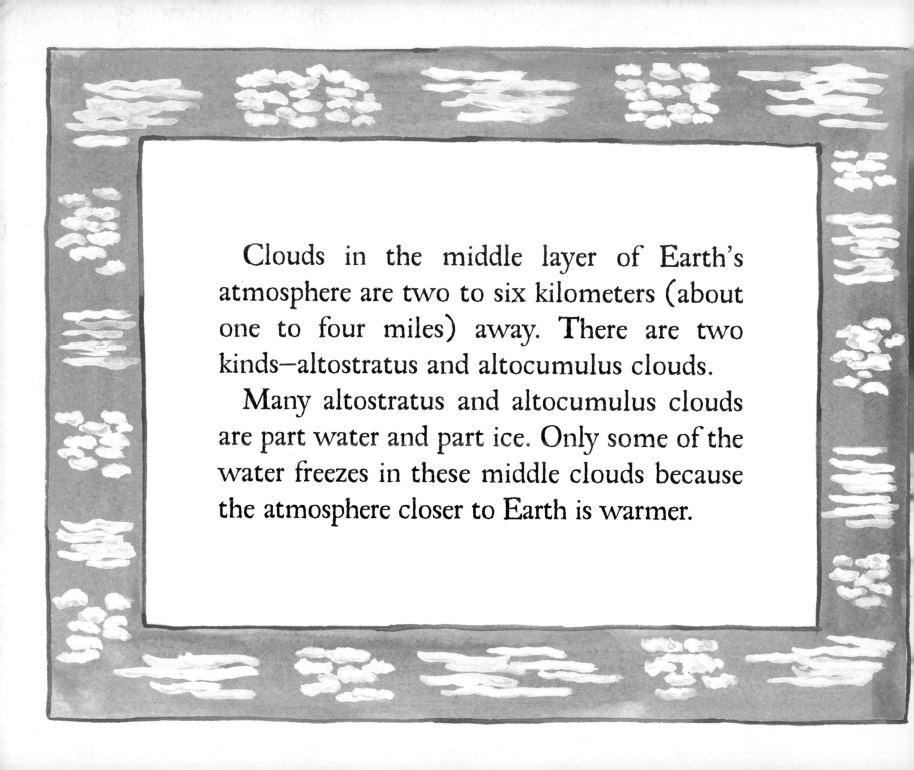

Clouds in the middle layer of Earth's atmosphere are two to six kilometers (about one to four miles) away. There are two kinds—altostratus and altocumulus clouds.

Many altostratus and altocumulus clouds are part water and part ice. Only some of the water freezes in these middle clouds because the atmosphere closer to Earth is warmer.

Cirrostratus

Cirrus

Cirrocumulus

Cumulonimbus

Altostratus

Altocumulus

Cumulus

Stratocumulus

Nimbostratus

Stratus

Altostratus clouds are gray-blue and streaky and cover the sky. They tell you it could rain that night or the next day.

Altocumulus clouds look like ocean waves—puffy,
white, and gray. If you see them on hot, humid days,
a thunderstorm will probably come.

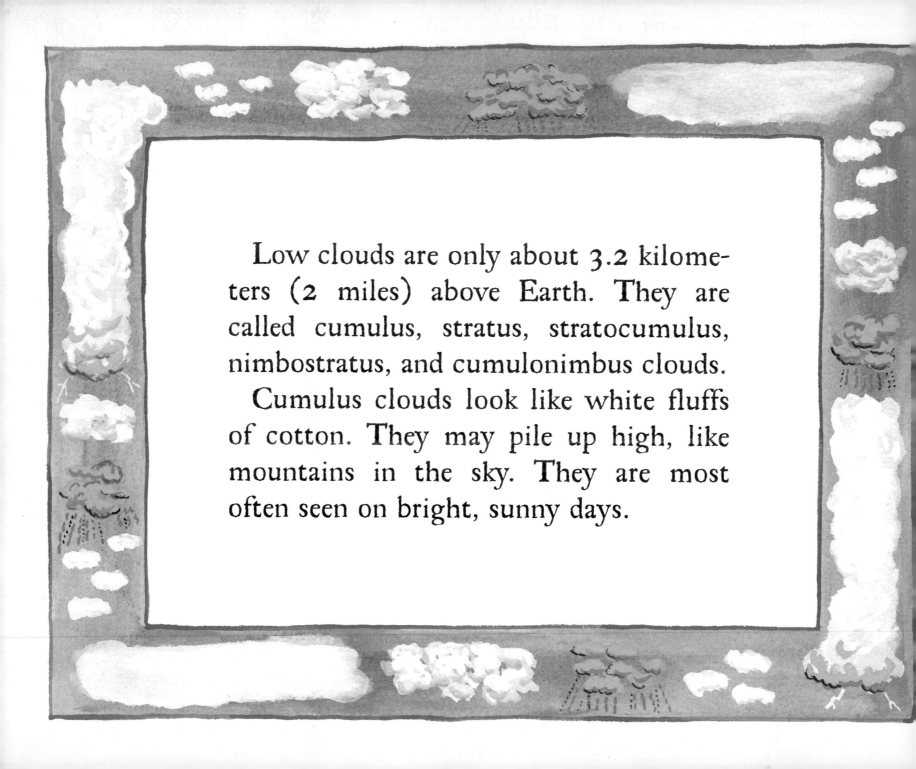

Low clouds are only about 3.2 kilometers (2 miles) above Earth. They are called cumulus, stratus, stratocumulus, nimbostratus, and cumulonimbus clouds.

Cumulus clouds look like white fluffs of cotton. They may pile up high, like mountains in the sky. They are most often seen on bright, sunny days.

Cirrostratus

Cirrus

Cirrocumulus

Cumulonimbus

Altostratus

Altocumulus

Cumulus

Stratocumulus

Nimbostratus

Stratus

Stratus clouds are gray and cover the whole sky.
They usually mean rain, but not much.

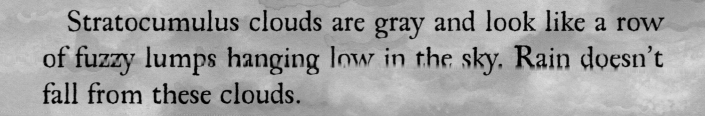

Stratocumulus clouds are gray and look like a row of fuzzy lumps hanging low in the sky. Rain doesn't fall from these clouds.

21

Nimbostratus and cumulonimbus clouds both tell you there will be very wet or even stormy weather.

"Nimbo" or "nimbus" in a cloud's name means it is a storm cloud. Nimbostratus clouds are dark gray and ragged looking at the bottom. Rain or snow falls steadily from them.

23

The scariest clouds are cumulonimbus clouds. If you are standing under them, they will look dark gray instead of white. Sometimes they look almost black. They seem to swell as they climb higher and higher into the sky.

If you see cumulonimbus clouds in the sky, you should run inside as fast as you can. They mean a thunderstorm is coming, and thunderstorms can be dangerous.

Sometimes balls of ice, called hail, fall from cumulonimbus clouds. Sometimes dangerous funnel-shaped tunnels of wind, called tornadoes, grow out of them.

If there were no clouds, Earth would be a very different place. Clouds are important to everything that lives and grows here. They bring the rain all plants and animals need.

If there were no clouds, there would be no rain. Nothing could live. If there were no clouds to hide the sun, Earth would become very hot during the day and very cold during the night. The temperature change would be too much for most plants and animals to live and grow.

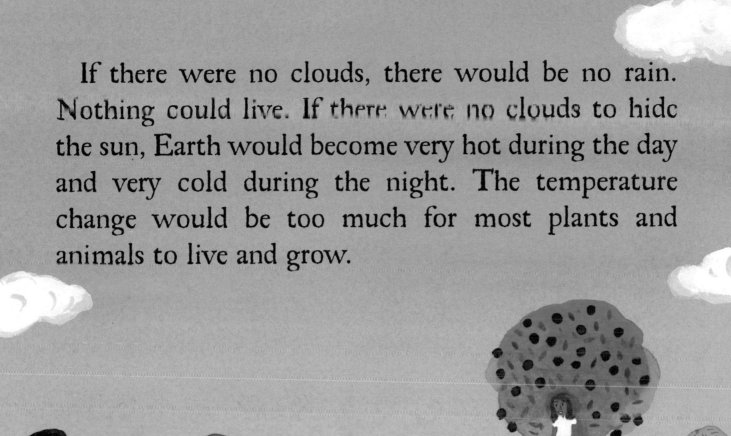

Sometimes you see more than one kind of cloud
in different parts of the sky at the same time.
That's because the wind is blowing away some
clouds and bringing in new ones. This means the
weather will change.

Now that you know which clouds bring rain or snow, which bring storms, and which bring sunny weather, you can tell in advance what the change will be. That's what scientists called meteorologists do.

More than half of Earth is always covered with clouds, even though you may not see any where you live. But somewhere else on Earth someone else is looking at clouds in the sky above.

31

Find Out More About Clouds

Cloud Facts

- In 1803, Luke Howard used Latin words to classify four different types of clouds. Today there are ten classifications of clouds, but they are still based on Howard's original words.
- One raindrop is made up of about one million cloud droplets.
- Clouds have a large effect on the heating and cooling of Earth. Clouds can block sunlight or trap heat from escaping the atmosphere. Scientists are studying clouds closely to see how they might tell us more about global warming.

Create a Cloud

In a just a few quick steps, you can create your own cloud. You will need the help of an adult for this activity.

Materials:

One large round rubber balloon

One clean, dry, medium-sized glass jar

One rubber band

Approximately 3½ tablespoons of water (You may have to experiment with the water level to get it just right, depending on the size of the jar. The water should just cover the bottom of the jar.)

One match

One regular flashlight (no pen lights)

1. Cut off the mouth end of the balloon and make sure it fits over the lip of the jar.

2. Make sure the rubber band will hold the balloon tightly to the jar, and then place the balloon and rubber band to the side.

3. Pour the water into the jar.

4. With an adult, light a match over the jar and then blow it out.

5. As quickly as possible, put the balloon over the mouth of the jar and secure the balloon with the rubber band.

6. Allow the jar and balloon to sit for 2 minutes so that the smoke from the match will disappear.

7. Turn off the light in the room.

8. Turn on the flashlight and place it near the jar.

9. Push down on the balloon for a few seconds and then quickly pull it back up.

What did you see when the balloon was pulled back up? Why do you think the small cloud formed? Did you notice the droplets of water on the sides of the jar?